# Gutsy Tales Off the Rails: Living Out Loud

Gordon, J. Blackwell, & Storytellers, *Gutsy Tales Off the Rails: Living Out Loud*

Copyright © 2018 by J. Blackwell Gordon, Pamela Rambo, Dorothy Erlanger, Yolanda Gray, Shanna Kabatznick, Shirley T. Burke, Elizabeth Louis, Joan Bowling, and Angela L. Edwards.

Published by KWE Publishing, P.O. Box 635, Prince George, VA 23875. www.kwepub.com. Contact at kwe@kwepub.com.

ISBN (paperback) 978-1-7321034-8-1

Library of Congress Catalog Number 2018954723

First Edition. All rights reserved. No part of this publication may be reproduced in any means, electronic or mechanical, including recording, photocopying, or any information storage or retrieval system, without written permission of the author. The exception would be in the case of brief quotations embodied in the critical articles or reviews, and pages where permission is specifically granted by the authors.

Although every precaution has been taken to verify the accuracy of the information contained herein, the authors assume no responsibility for any errors or omissions. The authors shall have neither liability nor responsibility to any person or entity with respect to loss or damage caused, or alleged to have been caused, directly or indirectly, by the information contained in this book.

Storytellers Channel
Contact Gayle Turner at info@storytellerschannel.com

www.kwepub.com

## Once Upon a Time...

Back in 2015, Mary Foley, a member of the National Speakers Association (NSA) Virginia and a former participant in one of Storytellers Channel's *Stories Matter! Workshops*, asked if we would donate a seat in an upcoming workshop for a fundraiser for NSA Virginia. We did, and Dorothy Erlanger, a member of NSA Virginia, had the winning bid for the seat.

Unfortunately, events transpired so that we did not hold a workshop that year. The following year, Joan Bowling, a member of NSA Virginia, called and asked if we would support the association again by making a similar donation. I felt badly about Dorothy's bid having won the seat and then the delay in her getting to reap the reward of her investment. So, I suggested we allow NSA to auction off not just a seat but an entire workshop. They could keep the funds they raised, and Storytellers Channel would keep the money from the door at the subsequent showcase. John Whitworth, Storytellers Channel Co-Founder, agreed and Joan Bowling, Shirley T. Burke, Angela L. Edwards, Captain Jim Gordon, Yolanda Gomez Gray, Elizabeth Louis, Shanna Kabatznick, and Pam Rambo joined Dorothy and we set a date to showcase their stories: Tuesday, November 29, 2016.

Starting in October, the participants met from 7:00 to 10:00 one night a week and worked on their stories.

The rehearsal process was straightforward. The participants were asked to tell their stories out loud once a day, every day, to someone. On workshop nights, they would stand in the front of the room, tell their story, and receive feedback. Due to my experience in writing workshops during college, I was very strict about the kind of feedback permitted. Those workshops had been akin to dropping fatted calves into pools of piranha; people seemed to feel they had to find something wrong with their fellow writers work to justify their place. And the more "brutally honest" they were, the better.

It takes guts to stand up in public and tell a personal story. Rumor has it that more people are afraid of speaking in public than of dying. And even though these members of NSA were experienced speakers, they weren't interested in public humiliation. And that included the rehearsal process; so, the only feedback permitted was the following:

1. What you specifically liked.
2. What you'd like to hear more about.
3. If you got lost in the story, where did you get lost and what didn't you understand.

That was it. Nobody was allowed to suggest changes to another's story. As is human nature, everyone seemed to want to, at one time or another, but they quickly caught on to the wisdom of the rules of the game.

From night one, we worked on structuring the stories. The goal was for the stories to last no longer than ten minutes each. Some were successful in this goal, others less so, but our primary goal was to structure stories in such a way that their family and friends would ask them to tell their stories again instead of rolling their eyes and praying they'd stop talking.

The participants were sent a PowerPoint, *Thoughts on Crafting a Good Story**, that laid out a process for editing their stories once they had spoken them out loud for the first time. The first brave tellers stood up and invariably apologized about their stories not being ready or good or whatnot. They had to be reminded that was why they were there and to stop stalling and share with us what they had. After the first few tellers had offered up their story in its nascent form and the floor hadn't opened up below them, and no one had scoffed or snickered or in any way demeaned anyone, they all got into the spirit and jumped in and played.

The tellers were encouraged not to write out their stories until after they had performed them. You may be wondering, "Why?" Once written down, the propensity is to try to remember and retell that which has been so painstakingly wordsmithed. You may be thinking, "What's wrong with that?" Well, the goal is to share the "movie" the storyteller is seeing in their head with their audience so they can share the experience. Reciting a memorized text, unless you're a trained actor, frequently results in a stilted performance. The teller becomes so involved in remembering that they lose their connection with their audience.

The stories in this anthology have been transcribed and edited from the videos of the showcase performances.

As the weeks progressed, so did our tellers' mastery of their stories, and their comfort and confidence telling before this, their first audience.

Up until this time, *Storytellers Channel's Stories That Matter!* Showcases had been held at Richmond Triangle Players' theater. Unfortunately, they were booked, and we had to find another theater. I had been volunteering with Henrico County's Economic Development Authority for several years and in a Business First meeting I met Kevin Liu. After serving as an officer in the Marine Corps, Kevin was now running The Tin Pan, a music venue in Richmond's fashionable West End.

The night of the performance that had seemed a long way down the road when we began was suddenly upon us and with it came attacks of nerves. Did I mention it takes guts to risk humiliation by standing up and telling a story in public? It seems no matter how many times you've stepped before an audience, even the experienced among us feel jittery when the pudding gets put to the proof. Some of the tellers confided in me later that they had been so anxious they had considered not performing. But in the end, this was an invited audience of family and friends. They felt compelled to support one another and so fortunately they all showed up. And you'll forgive me for being a bit biased as their director, I think they were delightful. And you can judge for yourself because Mary Foley and her partner, Bill Eastman, volunteered to video the performance. Those videos may be viewed at StorytellersChannel.com/storytellers.

Well, the night flew by and everyone in the audience had a grand time. My mother was there, applauded the tellers, and gave me high praise for my work. And let's face it, I don't care how old you are, who doesn't want praise from their mom?

Time passed, and Shirley T. Burke reached out to me and said, "Remember how we wanted to transcribe our stories and publish them?" I said, "Yes." And she said, "I want you to meet Kim Eley of KWE Publishing." Well, we met, and this book is the result of that meeting.

I never tired of listening to these stories during our rehearsals, nor during their performance at the Showcase, nor when I watch them on *Storytellers Channel*; as such, I feel confident that you, too, will enjoy them as you read them here, watch them online, or if you're truly blessed, get the opportunity to hear them in person. You know all of these speakers/authors/storytellers are available to speak and *you* can book them. You'll find their contact info at the end of their stories.

Until then, enjoy!

*Gayle Turner is Co-Founder of The Storytellers Channel, Inc. and serves as its CEO. He currently serves as the President of the Virginia Storytellers Alliance, the state trade association for storytellers. An acclaimed performer with over 60 years' experience on and behind the stage and screen, he is also an accomplished entrepreneur having started his business career when he bought his first business at the ripe old age of ten. (That's a story you'll have to ask him to tell you when you meet him.) He is available to speak and can be reached at Gayle@StorytellersChannel.com.*

*Storytellers Channel produces among other things the Hearts Afire Storytelling Festival, the Mountain Mack Virginia Liars Contest and Stories Matter! Workshops and Showcases.*

*\*To request a copy of Thoughts on Crafting a Good Story, email Info@storytellerschannel.com with "Thoughts PPT Request" in the subject line.*

## Table of Contents

*Pam Rambo - The Queen of the Second Row* ................................... *1*

*Dorothy Erlanger - The Next Hundred Yards* ................................... *7*

*Yolanda Gray - The 24-Hour Woman* ........................................... *15*

*Shanna Kabatznick - How Did I Get Here?* ..................................... *19*

*Captain Jim Gordon - Searching for Treasure* ............................... *23*

*Shirley T. Burke - Have You Been to Selma Today?* ..................... *29*

*Elizabeth Louis - The Gift of Africa* .............................................. *37*

*Joan Bowling - What Makes a House a Home* ............................. *45*

*Angela L. Edwards - Wonderland* ................................................ *51*

*References* ................................................................................... *59*

My mama was a Methodist; she had ways. The word "impossible" was not in her vocabulary. She believed that anything worth doing could get done...with enough effort. My dad, on the other hand, was a Presbyterian. He believed in predestination and that however his children turned out was "how the Lord intended." So, if you talked bad about his children, you were talking smack about Jesus.

So, with this semi-dysfunctional protestant family background, I invite you into the way-back machine to Sedgefield Elementary School in Newport News, Virginia, in 1957. There's a meeting going on in the principal's office and it's about me; on account of I wasn't normal. My mama didn't want to be there because she said they didn't raise me to be normal in the first place.

I was instructed to visit the principal's office by my second-grade teacher, Mrs. Garrett, who was six-foot-one and had a very low voice. She told me to gather all my things and go to the office. She was very serious all the time and kind of looked like a prison warden.

I did not question the apparent get-out-of-school-free card, thinking that I had probably forgotten a dental appointment and was about to get the afternoon off. I would have rather gone to the dentist than school, any day. When I showed up at the principal's office, Principal Douglas and both of my parents were there. My parents were in their Sunday clothes and that was NOT a good sign.

Somehow Mrs. Garrett magically appeared in the principal's office (I don't know how she got past me in the hallway). My first-grade teacher, Mrs. Little, was also in attendance. Now, Mrs. Little was aptly named because she was not much taller than a first grader. Poor Mrs. Little was afflicted by spending one year trying to teach me how to read and write. This caused her to develop a nervous tick in her neck and continually twist an imaginary hanky in her hand.

Shortly after I arrived, I was instructed by the principal to sit quietly, which I did in my Mary Jane patent leather shoes and my starched pinafore, proudly holding on to my Cinderella lunchbox. Now I didn't understand much of what was going on. I just knew I wasn't in class, so that was pretty good. When Principal Douglas started the meeting, she welcomed my parents and told them "we are going to have this meeting because little Pamela is abnormal and we should talk about her future." That's how my teachers talked at that meeting, like I wasn't really there. I always thought it might be fun to be invisible.

The principal first introduced Mrs. Little, who confessed that she had socially promoted me in first grade because she couldn't take another year. She went on to explain that I was "a willful child, writing R's backwards and mangling the Mother's Day ashtray art project." Apparently, I made a poorly constructed clay accessory-of-early-death for my parents.

Mrs. Little's verbal dissertation ended with her explanation about how "going home had also been a problem" because when she instructed the second row to get ready for the bus, "everybody went to the coat room, but Pamela." The second row would come back and give me my coat, help me put it on, pack up my bookbag, hand it to me, and help me off to the bus. That was very disturbing to Mrs. Little. Now, from my point of view, I saw it totally different. I was the Queen of the Second Row. They worked for me. I trained them to get my coat and pack up my bookbag. I had management potential and most managers ARE a little abnormal.

Then Mrs. Garrett got up and she said that she "didn't think I was willful at all" as a second grader. Not that I understood what willful meant. I was just sitting there in a chair that was way too tall for my legs and my patent leather shoes, swinging my legs, waiting to go home. Now, Mrs. Little and Mrs. Garrett both had two-year normal school diplomas. They were very educated people and, in her research, Mrs. Garrett said she had found "similarities in mental retardation to Pamela's behavior and thought that there was not a willful issue. There was a lack of ability issue." And then, Mrs. Douglas said, "as you can see, we are in agreement that you should take little Pamela home and not have her come back to school."

To me, as a seven-year-old, that was the best idea ever! How cool was that? But my joy was squashed by my Methodist mother who thought all things could be accomplished if you worked hard enough, and she said, "thank you very much for your input, but we didn't raise Pamela to be normal and we'll just let her continue to come to school." I'm sure that made Mrs. Garrett think: *Social promotion. Definitely social promotion.* My parents went away and I thought, okay, that's the end of this. I was not happy to have to stay in school for the rest of that day. It seemed a waste to take all my things back to my classroom for the second row to pack up for me.

When I got home that afternoon, ready to play, I found that my mother had been very busy with her Methodist self. She had turned our home into a quiz show, a very bad quiz show. There were flash cards taped to the mirrors and the walls. There were posters everywhere. I later wondered how my daddy shaved during that period of time. The worst episode of the quiz show took place at dinnertime. As we passed serving plates my mother would say, "well, how many peas would you like? Let's count them out." After dinner, I thought the worst was over; dessert was coming, things were going to get better. Nope. Before dessert, Mama would say, "Oh, Pamela, we've got a surprise for you. Tell her Daddy, you tell her what the surprise is." Then my dad would say, "Okay. Pamela, will you spell chocolate for Daddy? If you can spell chocolate correctly for Daddy, we'll give you another scoop tonight."

Well, actually I did learn to spell chocolate and their bad quiz show worked. Over time, my grades (and my dress size) did increase and I went from the turtle reading group to animals that are a little faster. There were bumpy rides through the rest of school, but I did get pretty good at writing. One teacher asked my mama to stop writing my papers and Mama had to explain to her, "I don't write her papers." Now math was another matter.

My parents didn't raise me to be a normal person because they wanted me to have the chance to become extraordinary. I later became a road scholar, having attended most of the colleges off of the interstate 64, and actually graduated. Isn't that amazing?

The secret to the story of my unlikely success, as a girl with dyslexia in the 1950's, was my Methodist mama who believed in me and my Presbyterian daddy who was quietly proud of me no matter how I turned out. The confidence of my parents rubbed off on me. It was reinforced by a saying that I heard from my mama from the time I was a little girl all the way through college:

*You're special. There's nobody like you and there's nothing worth doing that you can't do.*

There are three important lessons from this story of the dark side of education vs. the wisdom of loving parents. The first lesson is: never mess with a Methodist mama. The second lesson is: don't talk bad about a Presbyterian man's children. And the third lesson is: always tell your children that they're special, that there's nobody like them and that there's nothing worth doing that they can't do.

Pam Rambo was a dismal failure at ashtray making in first grade pottery class. To further shame her family, she was a charter member of the turtle reading group and unable to successfully *solve for x* in seventh grade. If SOL tests were given back when she was in school, she'd have been SOL.

In a bizarre turn of events for a dyslexic kid who hated school, Pam went to four colleges and graduated with five degrees. They never asked her if she had learning differences; she never revealed that information. (They can't take a doctoral degree back, can they?)

Focusing on the natural gifts of students and helping them realize their dreams, Pam started a successful educational consulting firm in 2010. When she is not busy helping students succeed, she entertains audiences with amusing tales about the lessons adults learn from students.

757-903-6511
ramboresearch@gmail.com
www.ramboresearchandconsulting.com

How old were you when you learned how to swim? Well, I was four! I had learned how to swim that summer and was so proud of myself. My family was vacationing at Lake Michigan, and this day was even better because I had Mom all to myself. Daddy had gone into town with my brothers so there was no competition – just the two of us.

I'm out in the lake swim, swim, swimming - looking up to make sure Mom's still there.

Swim, swim, swim, "Mom, are you still there? Oh! Oh! I can't touch. Oh no. Oh no. I'm going down!" The next thing I feel is Mom's hand on my shoulder pulling me up out of the water. I'm now sitting on the sand, wrapped up in a towel, warm and safe.

What happened? I had been swimming in circles. Due to a birth defect, my left arm is longer and stronger than my shorter, weaker right arm, which makes it difficult to swim in a straight line. As I swam, I was gradually working my way into deeper water.

Now, most parents would yank the kid out of the water saying, "Don't you dare go near the water again." My parents were different. They yanked me out of the water, made sure I was okay, and enrolled me in a swim class!

But wait, there's another problem. How does a swim instructor explain to me how to swim straight? They don't have any arm-length difference swim experience. I basically taught myself via "head whacks." Paddle, paddle, paddle until your head hits the side of the pool. Then paddle, paddle, paddle until you whack against the side of pool yet again. I gradually started to swim straight, just by figuring it out for myself. I learned that the 'figure it out' approach worked with many other challenges in life. It became my normal in career and personal life track. Don't worry if no one else has done this, just take it on and figure it out.

Moving forward, I grow up, go to college, start a career and a company and then all of a sudden in my late 40's, I'm up against the ultimate obstacle - ovarian cancer - with no history of cancer in my family. Now, I tend to be 'Miss Independent' and handle every challenge on my own, but this is one you don't want to face by yourself. You ask questions, you keep yourself healthy, active and informed, take your chemo dosages, lose your hair, trust your doctor, and rely on your support network. We eventually got through it with my hair coming backing in gray and curly!

Was I feeling victorious? No, actually I was feeling very depressed. I didn't understand this. I had gotten through my chemo, the vital numbers were on target and here I was, curled up in a ball of depression. I could barely get out of a chair. What I didn't realize at the time is that this is actually normal. After you finish up chemo, you're no longer <u>doing</u> something about the problem and that is very scary.

One day I'm sitting just reading our local Richmond Times-Dispatch newspaper, when I see a notice about training for a mini-triathlon for the 50's crowd. Okay, so the age fits. Let's see. I could swim 300 yards in a pool. I had my old college bike hanging somewhere in the rafters and could probably work up to the 12-mile race distance. I could maybe walk the 5k 'run' leg to finish up. No way could I run it!

Hmm…maybe having a goal to work towards would help get me out of my total funk. I signed up for the training. I joined a group of fellow 50ers, but not thinking about it as a training 'team'. I got into the group for <u>my</u> feelings, for getting <u>me</u> out of <u>my</u> ovarian cancer depression. What I found was an unexpected plus from a totally supportive group of people. Ability and age didn't matter. No one cared if you were first, last, or in the middle. This group was rooting for you. The coached guidance and practices were fantastic, but the best was the interchange with others in this amazing group.

The day of the event, I got out there and did the 300-yard pool swim (with a straight black line painted down the pool bottom for the swimmers to follow) and pedaled the 12-mile bike ride with ease (biking is my strongest event). I did walk most of the 5k distance, but who cares about speed – I finished the race! What a feeling of triumph!!

I'd gone into this event thinking, "I'll do one and that will be it." Wrong. I was hooked and started doing more and longer triathlons. The next thing I know it's about five years and many races later. I'm on the shore of Lake Mead, Nevada, to do a National Champion Triathlon, an event including a 1.2-mile swim, 56-mile bike ride, and a 13.1-mile run.

The first thing one has to do in preparing for a race is get familiar with the course by driving the bike and running courses. Usually I take my "Sherpa," husband Bob, along, but he was back at the farm taking care of the dogs and horses, so this time I rented a car and drove the course myself. I'm driving along and pretty soon the road goes up through the mountains — really high and really steep. As the road rises, my stomach is dropping. I'm saying to myself, "there is no way, no way I can bike this course."

I got back to the edge of the lake and called Michael, my trainer in Richmond. "Michael, I'm not doing to do this. I'm not starting. I can't do this. The hills we trained on in Hanover County are not the mountains outside Las Vegas, Nevada."

Michael said, "Dorothy, calm down. You are trained for this. You cannot look at this course by looking up at the mountain top. You have to look at just the next 100 yards right in front of you and figure out how you are going to manage that next 100 yards."

"Alright, Michael, Okay, I'll start," I said with about zero confidence that I would succeed.

I got out there the next day on that 'impossible' bike course and you know what? *The Next Hundred Yards* mindset worked amazingly well. I got through the mountainous part I had driven, back to the edge of the lake. However, I had forgotten the last six miles went from the lake front up to the town in the mountains where my bike was parked. All uphill. The road got progressively steeper and steeper as I went. However, by that time I was so ingrained into *The Next Hundred Yards* mindset such that I made it through and up over the last 9% grade!

Off the bike and into the run, I completed the half marathon run to finish the race. Beyond just finishing, I placed and qualified for Team USA, later competing at a world championship level — from a base of "can't do this, won't even start."

Then an even bigger challenge. I got talked into competing in an IRONMAN® triathlon — a 2.4-mile swim, 112-mile bike ride and a 26.2-mile marathon run — to be held in Coeur d'Alene, Idaho. I trained with an enthusiastic team, with the constant attitude 'of course you can do this'. Very positive, always team-focused. However, a couple of red flags were there that I didn't pay much attention to. First, I had no coaching on the swim, just assigned drills/distances. Second, there were identical workout plans/distances for all ages, experience levels, sexes. Hey, no problem, the 'of course you can do this' mantra was always there.

I'm at the race, ready to go. I start the 2.4-mile swim, in 58-degree water and a scrum of swimmers, but gradually get sorted and on my way. My mind is already thinking about getting this out of the way to get to the bike. At the end of the 2.4 miles, I get out of the water ready to head for the bike. An official stops me, physically turns me around to face the timing clock – and tells me I have missed the swim cutoff time by one minute. ONE minute! They stripped the timing chip off my ankle. As I went practically crawling across the beach, over the loudspeakers I hear my name announced to the thousands of spectators as having missed the swim cutoff and couldn't continue the event. Humiliation on top of devastation. Never again! No way. I'm too old. I should never have done this race in the first place.

HOWEVER, this experience stuck with me like a nagging piece of unfinished business. I needed to compete again. I asked my coach if he could train me to complete an IRONMAN®.

"Absolutely," he said. "We will work a lot on the swim, and not over train on the bike and run. Enough to do the distance, not overdoing for your body"

"Okay, coach, I'll take it on." In making that commitment, I had three things going for me:
1. A top-quality coach who I trusted — and who really understood what I had to deal with, my specific challenges.

2. A *small* network of support, close friends plus "Sherpa" husband Bob who encouraged me all the way. *Not* the big rah rah "Of course you can do this" group. There was no "of course" about it and that chorus would have simply made me less confident.
3. An absolute commitment that whatever my coach said I needed to do was going to happen.

This time I hit the water, at IRONMAN® Maryland, with commitment and a driving focused mindset, attention in the moment only to what I was doing at that moment. I climbed out of the water 25 minutes <u>before</u> the cutoff time. I crushed the bike course of 112 miles in just over 6 hours. Next came the 26.2-mile Marathon run. That's really tough after doing the swim and bike parts of the triathlon, but I took it on 100 yards at a time. That mind focus got me though the Marathon run. I finished the IRONMAN® triathlon and was awarded my finisher's medal as the loudspeakers boomed, "Dorothy, you are an IRONMAN®!" What a thrill and accomplishment!

So, when you are thinking of taking on something new, ask yourself, 'What do I need to start? And to continue to the end? What's my network of help? What is the mindset I need and how do I build that? For me, support, coaching and *The Next Hundred Yards* mindset made the difference!

Never mind what age you are, or the challenges or obstacles you face. You can take it on. No matter what, no matter when. Start your next hundred yards at a time journey!

    Dorothy Erlanger inspires others to take personal charge of their wellness and their life decisions. Whether overcoming a birth defect as a child, launching a successful international business at 30, or beating cancer at 50, Dorothy is a master at getting through, around, and beyond challenges. And she loves sharing stories, ideas, tips, and enthusiasm. Her signature "*The Next Hundred Yards*" approach resonates with audiences in life-changing ways. Dorothy shows how each individual can conquer their own personal challenges, no matter what and no matter when they start.

    Dorothy lives what she inspires others to do. Having a birth defect actually proved to be her catalyst to success. Figuring out things on her own became her only normal and taking on big goals was only part of the picture. Her 'just take it on' approach helped as she overcame ovarian cancer, usually a life-ender. But surviving wasn't enough. Dorothy decided to become an athlete after 50 and has completed an IRONMAN® Triathlon — 2.4-mile swim, 112-mile bike and 26.2-mile marathon.

    In her corporate career, she was the first woman hired in an all-male industry and the company's first woman sent to Brazil as an executive. Off to a fast start, she learned Portuguese in a matter of six months while managing her Brazilian marketing staff to such success that she launched her own consulting company, working in 45 countries helping to improve marketing methods and facilitating management planning and decision-making. Perhaps the best testimony to Dorothy's impact comes from a corporate vice president: "Dorothy Erlanger is a superb speaker, trainer and teacher. A straight shooter. She is an impact person!"

As a lifelong spectator turned triathlete, Dorothy inspires others to move from 'victim' to 'victor'. Her story is living proof that finding a goal and a support team can transform the impossible into mini-steps that are possible, no matter when you start. Dorothy has been honored by the people she has served, being awarded the National Association of Women Business Owners Vanguard Award as well as many other awards.

Dorothy faces life's challenges with intensity and a witty, balanced approach that makes her message come alive. Whether taking on a mountain-sized goal or starting with her "mini-hacks for health," each person takes away powerful messages with lasting impact.

www.dorothyerlanger.com
O: 804.749.4100
C: 804.928.8232
de@dorothyerlanger.com

"I can bring home the bacon, fry it up in the pan, and never let you forget you're a man."

Remember that commercial from the eighties? That song would go on and on about everything that this woman could do. There wasn't anything that she couldn't do. As the song continued to play, out would walk this tall, blonde, beautiful woman in four-inch heels, holding the frying pan in one hand and clutching a fistful of dollars in the other. Then the camera would pan over to her two well-behaved children staring adoringly at their Mama, clutching a book, and waiting for her to come and read them a bedtime story. Then it panned over to her husband who was also looking at her adoringly, lovingly, and lustily.

The camera would come back to this woman and she'd have this look on her face like, "Yeah, that's me. I can have it all. I do have it all. I am that woman."

And then the narrator sealed that statement with the name of the perfume "for the 24-hour woman." And I thought, yes, this is who I want to be. I want to be that 24-hour woman.

Of course, back then I wanted to be anybody except who I was. I grew up in the late sixties and most of the seventies. Women were beginning to come out of their homes to pursue their careers and their education. They were leaving children at home and at daycares, and that's what I just fell into. Cosmopolitan™ magazine told us how to do it; we even had our own version of Playboy™ magazine. Remember Playgirl™? Yeah.

So, I started that journey of having it all. I had those two children. I had a husband who worked very hard, but he traveled all the time. I had a beautiful home, which was spotlessly clean every day. I went to school to finish my education. I worked full-time. That was my life. It's really hard work being a 24-hour woman.

What they don't tell you is that she doesn't sleep. And, you can't get it all done. So, I began this relentless exhausting and overwhelming task of having it all. It didn't work out too well. I was failing at this being a 24-hour woman.

I developed a daily routine that seemed to work for me. I would come home from work and kick off my heels. You know I wore heels because that 24-hour lady wore heels. So, I wore heels. I'd take off my jacket and go into the kitchen to make dinner for that evening--my night was just starting--but not before I went over to the kitchen cupboard, opened the door and pulled down my wineglass. Then I'd walk over to the refrigerator, open the door, and hit the spigot on my cheap box of white wine. I also had a jug of cheap red wine under the sink because I never wanted to run out. It was the only relief I could find on this hamster wheel that had become my life.

Well, at some point down the road, I crossed that line from needing that relief every night to the dark depths of alcoholism. I was emotionally, spiritually, and physically done, and I wanted to die.

One day, I don't know why (I call it a miracle), I woke up one morning after a three-day hangover, unable to go to work because that wasn't happening anymore. I was too sick most days. I just decided that I didn't really want to live this way anymore. I can't say why that happened. It was sort of miraculous. It gave me this little sense of hope.

I realized that I couldn't stop all on my own. I had tried to do that before; I was going to have to get some help.

I thought, "I'm going to call my friend." Now, prior to this, I had called this same friend. She was my drinking buddy and I had called her to come over and have a few drinks. That's what we did. We'd sit around and talk about our husbands, our kids and the world. I invited her over and she said, "Oh, I just got out of rehab and I'm not drinking anymore."

So, when I decided to reach out for help, I knew exactly who to call.

I walked across the street because I didn't want my family to hear me making that phone call. She answered the phone and I asked her for help. She said, "Yes, I will help you."

What I found out later was that what I had received that day was the gift of God's grace in my life.

It began to work in my life really quickly to free me, not only from the physical pain of my addiction, but also from the mental anguish and torment that I had lived with for so many years trying to be everybody but me-- trying to have it all.

Grace showed up in the women who came into my life to help me, to guide me on my path back to myself. It showed up in the doors of opportunity that opened for my healing. And it also came to live within me to give me the power to live it. Max Lucado says, "Grace is the gift that at the moment you decide to make a change in your life, gives you the power to pull it off."

So, can you really have it all? You know, I still struggle with that sometimes, but I like what Oprah Winfrey says. She says you can have everything you want; you just can't have it all at the same time.

Well, today, with this gift of grace, I have learned to love myself, to be okay with who I am, and to love others with God's love. And it has fueled a passion in me to help other women on this journey to find out who they really are, what they really want to create a life that really matters.

And I do this with God's help and His grace one day at a time.

Yolanda Gray works with professional and business women to guide them on the journey inside to get out of overwhelm, stress, chaotic thinking and destructive habits and finally take control of their lives with a fresh perspective for what matters most-- living life "out loud"—authentically and confidently-- in all that God created them for.

Her own path on the way to God and her life's mission started where many of the women she works with begin—feeling defeated, in despair—and desperately wanting happiness and love in their life.

Yolanda earned a Bachelor's degree in Human Development, a Master's degree in Human Relations and certified as a holistic life coach.

Through the years she shares the message that it's never too late to "Take Back Your Life" as a personal coach, in coaching groups, workshops and as a speaker to organizations, churches, retreats and private groups.

For more information, go to www.yolandagray.com.

So, I'm standing alone, I'm 18 years old and I'm wondering, "How did I get here?" Most importantly, it wasn't my choice. See, I was born and raised in Quito, Ecuador, to an American Jewish father and a beautiful Spanish Catholic mother. Very interesting combination. One thing that we did every summer is we would come to the United States and spend our vacation with my family and my grandparents. What I did not know was that this vacation was going to change my life.

My Dad and I were hanging out by the pool, having a good time, and he looks at me. He goes, "Shanna?"

"Yes, Dad?"

"Your mother and I, we love you very much. You know that, right?"

"Yes, Dad, of course I know that."

"Well, because we love you so much, we have decided that you're not going to continue this vacation with us. Instead, we have enrolled you in college here in the States."

I'm a little bit in shock and I'm looking at him. He sees that I'm in shock, so he continues, "Don't worry. We met some really nice people. They will get you all squared away and set up."

And then I'm going. So where was I going? And he says, "Starkville, Mississippi, Mississippi State University."

Mind you, I've never heard of that town. He sees me, and he goes, "Let me show you."

He pulls up the map. He's looking at it and he's looking at me and he goes, "It appears Starkville is too small. It doesn't have a dot on the map."

The next few days went like a blur. There was shopping, there was shipping, and there was saying my goodbyes. Before I knew it, I was on my way to Mississippi State University. And that's how I ended up in the lobby of Mississippi State wondering, "How did I get here?"

Fortunately for me, my roommate had true Southern hospitality. She took me under her wing and she showed me around. But people say there's culture shock, so I'm going to share with you three little stories that I think you'll find very interesting.

The first time I went out to eat is the first story. When we ask for a hamburger in Ecuador, we get a hamburger. When I asked for a hamburger here, they gave me a list of all possible toppings that can go on a hamburger. I was very proud because I knew English. I grew up bilingual. I did not, however, know Mississippian. It totally took me by surprise for the next week or two. Whatever they said I wanted I would just say yes because I didn't know what else to say.

Second, I learned on another occasion that my clothes were piling up. I asked my roommate, "When is the cleaning lady coming?" She looked at me and she said, "Grab your clothes. We're going to go find her."

I grabbed my clothes. We walked down the stairs of the dorm and I walk into a room full of washers and dryers. She says, "Here's some detergent. Here's some quarters. You just met her." I was in front of washers and dryers. I did learn how to do my laundry and I learned to embrace the color pink because whites and colors do not mix.

The funniest of all my stories happened when my friends decided that we were going to spend the summer in Washington D.C. They kept saying that it would be such a good thing for me to experience, especially because we were going to spend July Fourth at the Mall.

I kept on wondering, "Why am I going to go shopping on July Fourth and how are we going to watch the fireworks?" Well, when I got there, I figured it all out.

After college I did what I thought I needed to do. I found a job. I met someone, I got married, bought the house, had the kids, and lived happily ever after. Unfortunately, that ever after part didn't last as long as I thought and I found myself again alone thinking to myself, "How did I get here?"

But see, here's the thing. This time it was my choice. It wasn't my father's choice. It wasn't my friends' choice, and it wasn't my husband's choice. It was mine. I could choose to grab my kids, turn around, and go home. Or I could choose to grab my kids, look up, look straight, move forward, and walk into the unknown. That's what I chose, but I was still alone.

I was here, I was in Richmond, but I was still alone. And I figured that if I was alone, how many other women were needing that connection, that feeling of empowerment and strength? Hence the birth of FABwomen, a place that we've created. We've built a community of women who come together who embrace life, who are authentic, and who learn from each other so that we can grow both personally and professionally. So, looking back from a scared 18-year-old in a brand-new country, thousands of miles away from where I was raised, to the proud owner and founder of FABwomen, this has been a fabulous journey and it continues to be. So, I'm going to leave you with this: Next time you are in that place wondering, "How did I get here?" Remember, the choice is yours. What will it be?

As the Founder and Chief Empowerment Officer of *FABWOMEN,* Shanna Kabatznick is responsible for the vision, strategy and membership growth efforts of *FABWOMEN* as it expands across the country. Shanna is also the Owner and CEO of *Shanna K. – Making Money Fun,* where she coaches and works closely with women in helping them achieve financial goals so that they can live a bold, authentic, and impassioned life.

In 2014, Shanna founded *FABWOMEN* as an outgrowth of her natural passion and affinity to connect, educate, empower, and encourage women everywhere to become the best versions of themselves.

Born in Quito, Ecuador, to a Jewish American father and Spanish Catholic mother, Shanna moved to the United States where she attended Mississippi State University, receiving a Bachelor of Arts degree in Management Information Systems. As a successful business leader, professional speaker, professional financial strategist, presenter, coach, and trainer with over 20 years' experience in the finance and banking industry, Shanna has dedicated her career to helping women achieve financial health and freedom.

She is a speaker and author on topics of interest affecting women such as diversity, small business growth strategy, women and money. She has published articles in *CEO Magazine,* co-authored the book "Get It Done! Design the Business of Your Dreams," was interviewed at "Virginia This Morning," and has been a podcast guest with Sonabank P.O.W.E.R among others.

For more information, go to www.fabwomen.me.

In June 1972, I completed Virginia Tech's 5-year Cooperative Education program, graduated, and fell into a job recession. During college, I had worked for both the Defense General Supply Center and International Nickel in Huntington, West Virginia. I was working, making pretty good money.

In West Virginia, my mind went back to what I loved as a kid. I loved walking along the front shore of my grandfather's farmhouse searching for treasure. Sometimes, on a high tide, you'd find ware poles or corks from crab pots but you never knew what was there. So, it was exciting, searching for treasure.

After I graduated, there were no good jobs available. The bottom fell out. So, I thought, "Wow, what am I gonna do?" When one job didn't pan out and then another, I said, "You know what? I'm gonna do my childhood dream. I'm gonna sell Boston Whaler boats." I moved back to Richmond to the Bon Air house where I grew up with my mother and father and got a great job selling boats, bicycles, and snow skis in September.

Now, for those of you who don't know, there's not a lot of boat sales going on in September. I was working for Pinnell's Inc.; I had a whopping $65 a week draw against commission. I wasn't going anywhere fast on that. My brother, Rob, quit college, and he came moving into the bedroom we grew up in. We were acting like we were still in college.

At one point, our mother came to us and said, "I really hate to say this but I'm going to have to evict both of you."

My brother said, "It's OK, Mom. We got a house."

We had found at 7100 Jefferson Davis Highway, a 2-story house, slate roof, river rock fireplace, hardwood floors, for $160 a month. We thought we just needed two more guys, $40 a month rent. So, we did that. Moved in December. In March of the next year I looked out my bedroom window and saw in a small thicket of pines, ground covered in ivy, a perfect rectangle of jonquils. I thought, "Wow. How did that get there?" I mean, a perfect rectangle had to be somebody's design. So being curious, I thought I've got to find out more about this house.

On the back of the property was a tin garage with a little apartment attached to it where the gardener lived with his wife, the plumber. I began conversations about this house. He told me that house had been built for a madam who had five prostitute houses in Richmond during the Twenties. This was a beautiful house. I started thinking about that, thinking about this woman. I asked him more stories. The Depression hit. What man standing in the soup line can afford to spend money for time with a woman? She went out on Jefferson Davis Highway with a vegetable and fruit stand.

Jefferson Davis Highway is more commonly known as U.S. Route 1. U.S. Route 1 goes from Maine all the way to Florida. In the Twenties and the Thirties with the advent of the automobile, that was a great place to be. By the Seventies, the Interstate system had been developed. Interstate 95 from Richmond to Petersburg bypassed Jefferson Davis Highway. Old Jeff Davis Highway had fallen on much harder times. Motels were vacant, but the land was valuable, explaining why they gave us such a cheap rent. They wanted to hold that property and sell it commercially.

But, I kept thinking about the Roaring Twenties and that woman with five houses. There must be shoeboxes of money somewhere around on that property. Man, did I look.

I never found the shoeboxes of money, but I did make a lifetime friend out of one of my roommates. My brother got married there. I got engaged to a woman that I had an on and off relationship with during college. That was an interesting year.

Let's fast forward two years. I married. I bought the cheapest house in Richmond possible. For $16,000 in December, I bought a 43-foot fiberglass Nautaline houseboat. I moved aboard with my wife. It was magnificent.

We were in Varina, just downriver on the James River, at Tidewater Yacht Marina, just ten miles into downtown Richmond. I already had a job working for a major oil company. I said, "Life is pretty good!" I bought a red MGB GT sports car. I had a 13-foot Whaler with a 50 horsepower Mercury tied up on the stern of the houseboat. I thought, "Man! I got my treasure now! I'm making it! I'm buying it!" I remember specifically at one point looking up at the sky exclaiming, "I got this! I got this figured out!" Then, a bombshell hit.

The oil company said, "In about six months, we're going to relocate back in Houston Texas. Those of you who would like jobs, we'll be glad to transfer you to Houston, Texas." I thought, "Houston, Texas! I've heard they blow air conditioning out of the buildings to the cars. This doesn't sound like my kinda place." Not only that, it was going to be a lot further away from the Chesapeake Bay and the Virginia waterways I had grown to love.

I wrestled with the decision. Then a bigger bombshell hit, right before Christmas. I found out my wife was having two affairs at the same time. It flattened me. That was the worst Christmas of my life.

In January, I said, "Look. I'm sorry. I can't do this." We split up. I asked the oil company if they'd move me back onto a desk just so I could work all the time instead of thinking about my situation. That's what I did. After four months of depression, I was sitting in the forward cabin with a bottle of sleeping pills in my hand. I was ready to end the pain. Then I heard this still, small voice say, "Is this is the way you want it to end?" I thought, "No! I don't want it to end this way."

That's where I got the first real indication that real treasure came from that small, intuitive voice. For the next couple of decades, I started learning how to work with that. Some people call that intuition. I found that, when I did get the intuition, what if I did the other? Whoa! That was a big mess. So, a lot of stumbling and learning during those times.

Over the years, I learned to trust it. At another point in my life, I was working a day job in Richmond, going to church with my brother George and my nephew Daniel, singing in the church choir. Also, I was watching football in my rented bedroom in Chesterfield County. Really not a great life, but it was good.

What I'd never really had was that relationship that I'd been seeking. In December, I got this ***knowing***. I knew that the woman

I'd been searching for was out there. I knew that I just had to find her. A month later, we met in Louisa, at the Solid Grounds coffee shop. She was and is one of the great treasures of my life. I met a retired geologist who had moved back to Virginia from California to the Blue Ridge Mountains and loved to travel.

    The retired geologist is an interesting piece because, what do geologists do? They find all kinds of interesting treasure. We've traveled to the West Coast where she knew jade was on the beach. We traveled to Scotland where some of the oldest rocks in the world are. We cruised the Mediterranean, and many places in the Caribbean. My life became magical because I listened to that still, small voice. From a college party guy to an arrogant young man who thought he had all the answers, I had to be humbled. I learned that, within each of us, there's a small, still connection to that great intuitive voice.

Results Trainer for over 30 years and Chesapeake Bay Captain

"Within each person is the Seed of Greatness!"

*Songbook From My Soul, Notes of the Sea*, a collection of 50 poems, was published in 2012.

Captain Jim resides in a Mill Creek cottage on Virginia's Chesapeake Bay enjoying boating, sailing and kayaking. A love of the sea enriches his unique approach.

For more information, go to www.SuccessfulLifeSailing.com.

It was March 25th, 2006, a day that would be a red-letter day in my life for a couple of reasons. One reason was that I was at home alone and I had the remote control in my hands. I was going to decide what I was going to see that day on TV. I must have flipped from channel zero to channel 5,021. I was just looking to see what I'd been missing, but I still wound up on my same old favorite, Channel 32, Crime TV. I was introduced that day to two things. One was a documentary called "Home of the Brave." It introduced me to a lady named Mrs. Viola Liuzzo. L I U Z Z O. I'm going to spell it again. L I U Z Z O. I know it's in the program, but I want you to remember because I want you to look her up too. Why was this woman relevant, you ask?

Well, she's the only white woman who was documented that was killed in the civil rights movement during 1965. And why did it affect me so much? I had never heard of her. Never, ever heard of this woman. Let me tell you a little bit about her. She was a wife, mother, and a friend.

She and her husband lived in Detroit, Michigan, with their five children, three girls and two boys. She was sitting, looking at TV during the turmoil and all the violence in Alabama. She couldn't believe what she saw. She couldn't believe that this was her America. She just couldn't believe it. She was looking at that and then she heard Martin Luther King Jr. say, "It's one thing to send your money; it's another thing to come yourself."

With those words from Reverend King and the horrible treatment she saw people experiencing on TV, I believe she felt a strong need to do something. Well, when she heard about the four-day, 54 mile walk in Selma, Alabama, in support of the right to vote, when she heard about that, she packed her bag. She told her husband, "It is everybody's fight." Not just those people directly affected in Selma. That's when she got in her car and started a thousand-miles drive to Alabama. She arrived a few days later.

I told you that she was a friend. Her very best friend happened to be her housekeeper, a black woman named Sarah

Evans. They thought alike, they felt alike about so many things, and they were friends. They were true friends, true friends. They traveled to New York and other places, attending conferences and other activities that related to the civil rights movement. Ms. Viola even joined the National Association for the Advancement of Colored People, the NAACP. Can you imagine that? This was in 1965, y'all. Most people would be scared to do it now, much less 1965. I want you to know about this woman. Do you hear me? I want you to know about this woman.

I love what her children shared with me about their mother's friendship with Sarah. Sarah was the housekeeper; however, she and Ms. Viola did the work together. Yes, they did the housekeeping duties together. And then they would sit down, drink coffee, and talk. Yep, they were real friends. That friendship was so deep that Ms. Viola made Sarah promise that she would take care of her children if anything ever happened to her. That's how deep that friendship was. When Ms. Viola got to Selma, she did whatever was needed. She was a humble woman. If there were people that needed to be fed, she'd make sandwiches for them and the other volunteers.

If there were children that needed to be cared for, she took care of them. Another important duty she performed, even though it was a dangerous task at that time in history, was taking people back and forth to the polls to register to vote.

On March 25th, 1965, she was taking somebody home after working as a volunteer. A car pulled up beside her on Route 80 in Selma, Alabama. Someone in that car pulled a gun and shot her in her head. Fortunately for her passenger, they weren't injured. She wasn't as fortunate.

The story goes on. I decided I wanted to write a letter about this. I had to tell somebody about this. I had never heard of this woman. I didn't know anything about her. Somebody, somebody had to tell people about this woman. So, I decided, "I'm going to write a letter." I know some of y'all have said the same thing. Well, maybe you haven't said it, but I bet you probably thought about it, when you heard or saw something on TV, or heard something on the radio, or when you read an article in the paper. You've probably thought, "I'm gonna call that TV station," "I'm gonna contact that radio show," "I'm gonna to write to that editor." Does this bring back any memories about acting on something you have seen or heard on the TV or radio or read in the paper?

Well, it was days, weeks, months before I wrote that letter, but I wrote it. Hold on, I said letter, but it wasn't a letter. It was an email! You know, it is the 21st century. Yes, I finally wrote that email. I had gone online and looked up two people who had filmed that documentary. I wanted to tell them how much it changed me, how much it made me feel the depth of the pain, of what was going on down there in Selma, Alabama, during the Sixties. I wanted to know from them how they felt making the documentary, because I know it had to have had an effect on them.

Something else I didn't tell you, up until October 2017, for almost twenty years, I'd been doing a monthly radio show. It was called Women-On-Point (WOP)© on WCLM Radio©. Yes, we talked about a little bit of everything. It aired every first Wednesday of the month. Now I do a radio show every second Saturday of the month, 1:30 – 2:00 PM. In case you ever want to tune in, I am on Rejoice Radio© – 101.3 FM/ 990 AM / Rejoice 990.com

Well, I hit "send" on that email, the first Wednesday in July 2006. I hit send at fourteen minutes past midnight. There is another bit of information I didn't tell you. When I sent that letter off, that email off, I had attached a program that reflected what our radio show would be about that night and it was about three sheroes: the first black woman that ever got her pilot license, a native American, and Ms. Viola.

Also, in that email, I had written that I would love for her children to know that Ms. Viola was just as important in 2006 as she was in 1965. I wanted her children to know that as strongly as I did. I wanted them to know it. Well, let me tell you, I went to bed, got a little bit of sleep, got up the next morning, and as on all show days, my plate was full. I had work, I had errands, and I had a chiropractor appointment, so when I got ready to leave work that evening something told me to check my email. When I checked my email, there was an odd name there and that name didn't look familiar at all. So, I opened the email and it says, "if you get this before the show, call me and a number was there. My name is Mary. I'm Viola's daughter."

For some reason I forgot my back was hurting. I canceled the chiropractor appointment. I got in the car, went to the studio, and called Mary on my cell phone. I decided not to call her while I was driving because I knew I'd be crying like a baby and I would have been a hazard on the road. I just couldn't believe it. Well, I talked to her and she had let her sisters know about the plans to discuss Ms. Viola on the show. She got the information, I found out, from the director of the documentary. One of the producers I had emailed sent my email to the director and she sent it to the Liuzzo sisters. The sisters then decided they would follow-up with the person who had written the email.

Have I told you that I believe in the power of ONE? Have I mentioned that yet? Yes, I strongly believe in the power of one. You and me, I believe in that power of one. Yes, I do. Yes, I do.

Back to my story! I got to the station, I talked with Mary, cried, talked, cried, talked, and then I finally hung the phone up because it was time for the show to start. I went into the station and the very first call, the very first call we got says, "Hello, my name is Penny, I'm Viola's oldest girl."

Have mercy. It was wonderful, y'all. The show was wonderful. The conversations we had with both girls on the line were priceless. They told us about their mother's hopes, dreams, and desires. I learned so much more about Ms. Viola. It was a powerful interview and an unforgettable evening.

I checked my email at home the next morning. There was a letter from Ms. Viola's baby girl, Sally. Sally said she had missed the show and she just wondered if we had a tape that we could send her so she could hear what went on. I'm going to remind you here again that Sarah, the housekeeper and friend, had promised that she would take care of Ms. Viola's children. She did just that. She moved in, stayed at the Liuzzo home five days a week, with those kids, and she went home on the weekends, to her family. You hear me? Did I say that they were friends? Did I mention that they were real friends, not just so-called friends, but real friends? So, what happened? I'm reminding you of that because of what I'm about to tell you about Sally. I'm sure Sarah was just as hurt as Ms. Viola would have been, in the situation I share below.

Well, when Sally was six years old, she was stoned. S-T-O-N-E D, in case you didn't understand what I said. She was stoned in Detroit by adults. Adults threw stones at this six-year-old child. You hear me? She was stoned in Detroit by adults that called Sally a "nigger lover's baby." To a child that didn't even know what was going on. Six years old.

Over the past seventeen years, I've gotten to know these three women quite a bit. They have taught me a lot about their mother, but they also introduced me to something, an annual event, that is so important to them. The first week in March is when the riots, marches, hosing, and dog attacks of black people took place in Alabama. It is during this time that the term "Bloody Sunday" was the cry of the day. Some of y'all are old enough to know what that is and if you're not old enough, check Ms. Viola's story online. You get on a bus and they take you to these historical places, where things that have happened, bad things that happened in Selma and other parts of the state. I met the only little girl that survived the bombing in that church in Alabama. I got to talk with her. I met Congressman John Lewis who was beaten and jailed so many times. Because of this annual "Get on The Bus" trip, I have gotten to meet so many other local Alabama people that are sheroes and heroes. They matter!

However, the most important learning to me, after finding out about Ms. Viola, meeting her daughters, and meeting those other committed people in Alabama, was that it reiterated, it reinforced my belief in the power of one. And every day, every day that we are confronted with conflict and injustice, we are offered a choice. Every one of us, we're offered a choice. That choice is to either go to Selma or to NOT go to Selma.

So, I ask you, as I ask myself every day, "Have you been to Selma today?"

"Taking care of yourself IS NOT SELFISH, as a matter of fact I think it is a SPIRITUAL ACT OF KINDNESS." This is a personal quote by Shirley T. Burke, or "Shirley T" as she likes to be called.

She is a native of Goochland County and owner of the Esteem Institute, LLC. She is an Author, National Presenter, a Confident Coach, an EMCEE, Facilitator and a Radio and TV Host. She is a requested Corporation Presenter for businesses such as Patient First, Verizon, Local Governments throughout Virginia and various State Agencies, to name a few.

Until their program was discontinued, Shirley T was a regular presenter for Clemson University's Professional Development Program for Women. Her background includes a thirty-plus years career in public service, human resources, and the fitness industry. She holds a national certification as a PHR - Professional in Human Resources.

She was honored as the youngest Community Action Director in the United States in the early '70s. This is when she served as the Executive Director of the Powhatan/Goochland Community Action Agency, Inc, as part of the Office of Economic Opportunity, Office of the President of the United States.

She has been appointed by the Goochland Board of Supervisors to serve on the Goochland Planning Commission, the County's Easement Board, and the Youth Services Commission and other county organizations.

Shirley T is a member of the National Speakers Association (NSA) and the past-president of the Network of Enterprising

Women (N.E.W.) and the American Business Women Association - River City Express Network (ABWA-RCEN).

She was an honoree of Boomer Magazine's 2011 Top 10 IT List, where she is recognized as one of Richmond's most inspiring and influential people.

Her clients accuse her of being able to "push their follow-through button," which means they accomplish more than they ever dreamed they could. She considers herself to be an "apprentice of life" and is grateful to wake up each morning and report for duty. Some of those duties include being a wife, mother, grand and great grandmother.

She currently volunteers for a reoccurring nine-weeks "Livin' It Prison Project Program" at the Fluvanna Correctional Center for Women and the Chesterfield Diversion Center.

The core philosophy behind her life and teachings is the belief that **"each of us is here on this earth for a reason. No one can do what you have been sent to do. If you don't do what you have been assigned to do, it shall NEVER be done!"**

For more information, go to www.ShirleyT.com.

I was going to save Africa! You're probably wondering how I was going to do such a crazy thing. Well considering I was twelve years old, I didn't have much of a plan. In fact, I was more focused on the why. And the why was because one day when I was home sick from school I was watching "ER," but these weren't the typical "ER" episodes - these episodes depicted the horrors and the gruesome acts of the Congo army. Immediately I grew angry yet fascinated. I was angry because I couldn't believe that a human could treat another human in such demeaning and terrorizing ways, and I was fascinated because I was confused why I wasn't learning any of this in my world history class, so I did what I always do. I obsessed. I pulled out a notebook. I wrote "Save Africa" on the front and I put all of my research findings inside. I would carry this notebook around, to refresh my knowledge at any given point throughout the day, to remind myself of my new life's mission. I was going to Save Africa!

Jump forward twelve more years; I'm in my final stretch of college. I'm 24 and I'm two years behind the average four-year college plan - so to say I had senioritis was a bit of an understatement. I was three-fourths of the way finished with my very last quarter in television producing in Atlanta, Georgia. I came home to Richmond for a routine OBGYN checkup. Except this appointment was not routine. During the appointment, my doctor discovered a complex cyst on my right ovary. She consulted with a few other doctors and a leading oncologist who all advised me to stay home for the next two weeks to rule out cancer. Now, when the doctors first dropped the big "C", as you can imagine, a lot of things went through my head. However, I was a survivor! I had survived and overcome worse scenarios than this one. Therefore, I was determined I was going to defeat cancer if it turned out that way. The doctors also prepared me for the possibility of a full hysterectomy, in case they were unable to salvage my right ovary.

I was okay with the idea of a full hysterectomy because I was unsure if I wanted children, but what had me the most, what had me on my knees crying, is that I was 24 and I hadn't lived. I kept having this "I'll do it later" mentality. You know where you say things like, "I'll do it when I'm grown," "I'll do it when I'm an adult," or "I'll do it when the time is right." The issue with this limiting mindset is there is no good time to do anything. The time is now!

Doctors decided to schedule the surgery and when I woke up afterwards, I was told I did not have cancer. Now while I was blessed and happy, I was also very angry. I was frustrated because it took this emotional rollercoaster for me to realize I wasn't living as my authentic self. I knew who that was, but I didn't know how to relinquish her. I was unsure of how to be me and live as my authentic self without the worry or fear of what the world would say. I had spent all of my years up to this point trying to please other people, trying to do right by others, trying to survive, that I didn't know how to live right by myself. I wasn't living my life, but the life dictated onto me by the world.

In fact, I realized I was getting a degree I didn't want to do anything with. However, at this point, I was so close to getting that degree I was going to finish it. After recuperating from surgery, I headed back to Atlanta to complete the last two weeks of school and proudly graduate from the Savannah College of Art and Design (SCAD), Atlanta campus. One day while at home right after graduation, I came upon a Facebook post that said "wildlife documentary internship, South Africa." Immediately I grew enticed and I clicked on it. I investigated the program for the next few days, contemplating whether or not I should or should not apply. While considering what I should do, I continued to hear this voice that said, "Liz, you're going to apply. You're going to get accepted, and you're going to meet someone who's going to forever change your life." I was confused about why I kept hearing such a strong voice because I didn't want to do anything with TV or film, but I honored that voice and I applied. I wasn't too worried about the application process because I had graduated from a prestigious art school and I had a fairly strong résumé due to the university and my past.

Needless to say, I was accepted and the next thing I knew, I was halfway around the world in Mossel Bay, South Africa. I met my team and after a week and a half of planning we headed to the game reserve. I remember the excitement and hunger that overtook me when I arrived at the game reserve. Before we entered the actual reserve, we met our ranger, and got in our Land Rover.

Now, I will admit it – I was imagining a stereotypical Hollywood depiction of who my ranger was going to be and what he was going to look like. Well, I was wrong. Ettienne was early thirties, six-foot, strawberry blonde hair and very fair skin. After introductions, the team, Ettienne, and myself climbed onto the Land Rover and we entered the gates of the game reserve. Entering the game reserve was like a scene from Jurassic Park. All you saw were tumbling hills and animals roaming in their natural habitat, doing exactly what they were created to do.

I had gone to zoos before, but seeing animals, undisturbed, roaming with other animals in freedom, is absolutely breathtaking. It's a freeing sight. I had never felt freer than I did on that game reserve. The first thing we did after we entered the game reserve was we went and got situated at our campsite. Now our camp was in a literal bush. It was a bush that was large enough to fit three cabins, an outhouse, and an area to take a shower. We had no running water and no electricity. We used fire to keep warm and lanterns to see at night. The bush was used as a protector towards any curious or wandering animals that wanted to come in because nothing separated us from them.

After we got situated, we headed to go see the lions because there were about four cubs and at this time it was dusk. If you're familiar with house cats, they're quite lazy and predominantly more active as the sun goes down. After spending about an hour or so watching the lions be lazy, it was time for dinner. I decided to get in the front seat of the Land Rover and get to know Ettienne for two reasons. First of all, he had a gun! And, I'm in in the wild. I wanted him to like me enough to maybe save me prior to my teammates. Secondly, I was fascinated to learn more about the cultural gaps we shared. I was raised in a first world country. He was raised in a third world country and I was curious to know what that was like. After a few minutes of talking, I asked him a question that for the life of me I do not remember, but I remember his response. "Well," he said, "when divine intervention occurs…" I thought to myself "divine intervention?" I responded by saying, "You mean God?"

He said yes.

It was in that exact moment, I realized Ettienne was not only my ranger, he was my angel. He was the person I was supposed to meet. He was the person the voice spoke about months earlier, and that voice was God.

The remaining time I spent on the reserve that was meant for filming, I spent inside the Land Rover talking with Ettienne. For the first time in my life, I had the most authentic conversations. He saw me for me. He accepted me without judgment. He helped me to uncover a part of my life I had worked so hard to block out. Ettienne helped me begin the process of letting go and facing my traumas.

He explained to me the difference of what it meant to be spiritual versus religious. I was raised as a Methodist. Christianity was not new to me, but I was lost in my life. I was unhappy. I was surviving, not living. I was confused. It was in Africa that I realized I had spent so much of my life trying to survive – trying to just get to the next safe place in my life, that I didn't understand how to live. I especially had no idea how to live life in a spiritual manner. I didn't know how to thrive, and that's what I craved. I wanted to live a life with security, certainty, and where I could trust my higher power, my Father to protect and provide for me. I realized I had lived life where I had to be in control, where I didn't allow space for me to receive His grace.

I told Etienne that I had felt I had done so much wrong in life, that I wondered how God could ever love me, and Etienne said, "God loves you unconditionally." He continued to explained why it's so important to live obediently to the Lord. Due to the horrors of my past, I didn't trust easily. There were plenty of fleeting moments where I struggled to even fully trust Him, but then Ettienne explained that trusting the Lord is all you have because it's not your life and we live in a fallen world. It's His life that He has blessed you with. It's not your will be done, but let thy, God's, will be done. I had grown so connected to what it meant to live as a Christian that one night as I was fading in and out of sleep, this immaculate light came to me. The image started with a deep hue of gold trim followed by a transparent, almost cloudy white, accompanied by the most beautifully rich sky blue I had ever seen - and in the middle was Jesus wearing a robe, staring at me.

    At first, I thought I was crazy. I actually began to truly question my sanity. I rubbed my eyes and when I opened them, He was still there. As I looked at Him and He looked back at me, He raised His hand and He motioned me to follow Him. From that second on, I finally understood what it meant to follow Jesus, to lay your life down for His. It all clicked. I finally was able to fully surrender my life to Christ.

    I was so proud of myself that I decided to celebrate this victory with a baptism. But, where was I going to find a random pastor in the middle of the Savannah? Since I could not readily find any pastors to baptize me, I got creative. I baptized myself. How did I do this? I bungee jumped off the world's tallest bridge. I figured, what other way was there to show God that I truly trust Him with all of my being, beside relying on rubber bands and Velcro? I had been christened as a baby, but it wasn't my choice. It was my parents'. This time I was able to use my freewill and say to the Lord, "I AM LIVING FOR YOU, not for me!" If I had not gone to Africa, if I had not been brave enough to listen to that voice, and taken the leap of faith to travel by myself 10,000 miles away from my comfort zone to South Africa, I don't know if I would have ever received the enlightenment that I was blessed to experience. Since I was twelve years old, I have wanted to save Africa, but the irony is Africa saved me!

Elizabeth Louis is a personal and professional development coach who focuses on the significance of mindset and perception. She is an up-and-coming motivational and inspirational speaker, life-strategist, and warrior, who empowers people to live as one's authentic self. Her witty, direct, and transparent communication style educates individuals by showing them life is a choice. We can either CHOOSE to allow our brain and emotions to control us by reacting or we can choose to take control and respond, as we consciously desire.

Elizabeth believes success is a mindset and if a company or a person is not prospering then it is because of their thoughts, paradigms, and the perception that individual chooses to see. As a coach, she helps clients identify their paradigms and crush them by encouraging the individual to decide to remain in an empowering state of mind. She built her practice on the trinity of neuroscience, positive psychology, and the Biblical principles of success.

Elizabeth obtained her Master's of Science in Positive Psychology with a subspecialty in Coaching Psychology in September 2017. Her background is one that is quite complex and intricate. As a young child, she experienced a domino effect of death, extreme abuse, violence, an eating disorder that should have killed her, and other traumatic events. However, her invincible mindset led her to run her first business at the age of 13, become a professional model at age 15, move out at the ripe age of 16, and work on a wildlife documentary in South Africa at age 24 before entering the career field she arguably has done her entire life.

EMPOWERING INDIVIDUALS TO CHOOSE TO BE THEIR BEST!

For more information, go to https://elizabethlouis.com/.

Eighteen years ago, my husband and I were so in love, we would hold hands, take long walks, and talk about what we were going to do in the future. Eighteen years ago, we decided to get married. After that, we never saw each other because while we were crazy in love, we were also crazy to get married with four teenagers between the two of us. My husband brought a son and a daughter into the marriage, and I brought two teen daughters, and somebody always needed a ride somewhere. Band practice, homecoming, dance, football, game, church activities, sleepovers, friends' get-together, you name it. We were zooming everywhere. But when we did catch a moment to ourselves, it was the best.

Well, I'm pleased to report that all four kids graduated from high school and they're out on their own doing their own thing. And, for the first time ever in our relationship, it was just me, my husband, Roger, three empty bedrooms, two dogs, and all the time in the world to do whatever we wanted.

If we wanted to have beer and nachos and Reese's Peanut Butter Cups™ for dinner? Sure. No pajamas, no problem! Watch back-to-back Jason Bourne films all night long? Sounds like a good plan to me. We loved our carefree lifestyle. We would tell family, friends, and anybody who would listen about the fun that we were having, but then we made one fatal mistake. We told the wrong person.

This person was a dear college friend. Unbeknownst to us, she serves as a coordinator for an international high school student exchange program in the West End of Richmond, Virginia. Upon hearing the story, she said, "You know, Joan, we are in need of housing for international students this coming fall. Would you and Roger be interested in hosting one of those students?"

Oh my gosh. Well, you know, she's a dear friend. We wanted to keep her a dear friend. So, Roger and I talked, and we decided, sure, we would host a student. As long as it was a boy, he was a senior, and it was only a six-month commitment. She said,

"Sure. No problem." And in we welcomed Jennifer, a sophomore who would be with us for the next three years.

The truth of the matter is, we love Jennifer! She's smart; she's funny. She loves hanging with us. We loved hanging with her, getting to know her family, her customs, and some of her favorite foods. We would go out and about in Richmond and do a ton of really cool things.

Now as sharp as Jennifer was, again, she's in a new country and sometimes things will trip you up. For example, we went to CVS Pharmacy™ and we were standing in line. While you're standing in line at the counter, there's a ton of impulse items there. So, you have candy bars and you have gum; you have the People™ magazine. Will Brad and Angelina get back together again? And there's other impulse items over there. And Jennifer said to me, "Joan, what is that?" pointing to a small, square hot red breath strip.

And I said, "Those are Listerine™ breath strips in hot cinnamon. So, here's how that works. You pull out one of the breath strips, put it on your tongue, *wow!* You get this burst of hot cinnamony flavor. If your breath is a little stale, or if you have an interview and you want to freshen up your breath – these work great."

She said, "I will buy six of them."

I said, "That sounds great."

So, the next day Jennifer took the Listerine™ hot cinnamon breath strips to school with her. At the lunch table, seated with five Asian friends, she passed out a package to each one of them. And like synchronized swimmers, they pulled out a breath strip, put it on their tongue, and *wow!* They were hit with the shock of cinnamon! Like, "What just happened here?" Well, one of the teachers at the school saw the startled faces. She came over and just started cracking up when she found out what was going on.

We had a great sophomore year, the first year with Jennifer. That summer she returned back to China to hang at home before she came back for junior year.

Well, that summer, we ran into my friend, the coordinator for the International High School student exchange program here in the West End and she said, "You know, Joan, Jennifer's coming back for her junior year. You still have two spare bedrooms. Would you be interested in hosting a European student along with Jennifer?"

"Sure. We had a great time with Jennifer. Bring it on. No problem."

And we welcomed Ada. Ada was of Persian descent and lived in Germany. Now Ada was a sophomore and she was so excited, particularly because we had established some traditions welcoming Jennifer the previous year. One of those traditions was on a Friday night. If no one had any homework or, you know, wasn't too tired and had no sleepovers, we would vote on a movie, bring in pizza, chips, and drinks, and just chill in the rec room and watch the movie as a family.

It's the first Friday in September. We have everything laid out in the rec room. Ada comes bounding down the steps. Roger, my husband, and I are there and Ada says to us, "Joan and Roger."

We said, "Yes?"

She said, "I have news to share."

"Okay, what is it Ada?"

She said, "Jennifer, our Asian student. Jennifer has passed away."

"WHAT? She's dead?"

We drop the pizza and go running out of the room.

Ada goes, "No, no, no. Wait, wait, wait. I am wrong. I am wrong. Jennifer has passed out."

And I said, "Well, thank goodness she's still alive. But what is happening in that bedroom?"

So, we proceed to continue to walk. She was, "no, no, no wait. I am wrong. I am wrong. How do you say, 'willfully sleeping throughout the day'? Uh, Jennifer is napping."

So, we go from an international crisis to "I will be down in a few minutes to see the movie and eat some pizza."

That was Ada. We had a great year with her. And, as she was just here for a one-year commitment, she went back to Germany that summer. Jennifer went back to China after she had completed her junior year.

So, that summer, we run into our friend, the coordinator for the International High School Student Exchange Program. And she says, "You know, Joan, Jennifer's coming back for her senior year. You still have two spare bedrooms. Would you be interested?"

Yes. We know the drill. Bring it on!

So, this year we welcomed Emilia from Spain. And, when Emelia arrived in the United States, she arrived with a huge dose of confidence. This was one of our first conversations in the first two weeks upon her arrival.

"Joan. I know everything there is about the United States. I have studied your culture. As a matter of fact, I have spent three summers in Philadelphia at a camp for a week. I am good with America."

And I said, "Well that's really great. I'm happy for you and if we have any questions we'll certainly run it by you first for your input."

Two weeks into Emelia being here, Jennifer returned as well. Their school hosts an international luncheon at BJ's Restaurant™ just down here in Richmond's West End on a Saturday. There's about 50 of us. You have administration and faculty from the school. You have members of the program, parents, host families, and kids. It's great food and conversation, short talks, everybody's networking, getting to know each other and then it's time to wrap up and leave. Well, Roger and I had taken two separate cars.

I'm going to take the girls, Jennifer and Emilia, to run some errands and my husband Roger is taking the second car. Emelia finds out about this and she says, "Joan, why Roger no drive with us?"

And I said, "Well, he's going to go home and smoke a chicken." She said, "How does he fit it in his mouth?"

We have these and so many great stories from our international kids. But this particular story started off with two middle-aged people falling in love and creating a new family with their extended kids. The love story continued with the hosting and the welcoming of our international students. Thanks to our international kids, we fell back in love with Richmond, our city, our culture. We did things we hadn't done for decades like go to a University of Richmond basketball game or attend the Richmond Ballet. We go see exhibits at the Virginia Museum of Fine Arts or just stroll Carytown. Thanks to the international flavor of our extended family, we came back home again.

Joan Bowling is a top communications trainer, speaker, and presentation coach. She is a skilled teacher and loves the spoken word. Her witty style and easy communication inspire others to make the changes they need to perfect their pitch, to create memorable messaging, and make more profitable presentations. And, isn't that what it's all about? Joan helps you get results.

Joan is also passionate about the world of sales and that passion for sales was recognized with a coveted Sammie award for broadcast sales. She is a five-time Sterling Club winner for direct marketing sales and was twice nominated as the National Association of Women Business Owners' (NAWBO©) Member of the Year/Richmond, Virginia.

Joan has served as President of the National Speakers Association (NSA) Virginia state chapter and is the recipient of the coveted NSA Virginia Idol Virginia award. A Toastmaster© since 2015, she earned First Place in the 2018 Toastmasters© District 66 International Speech competition. One of her joys is working with TEDx© clients to craft their short stories of inspiration to share with many.

Joan's career includes two decades in broadcast sales, live television hosting for ten years, and being co-founder of a successful Richmond advertising agency.

Thanks to her parents, Joan was blessed with "a good set of pipes! And, having done voice work for decades, you may "bump" into her voice in the Commonwealth on a radio commercial or at a gas pump.

For more information, please go to www.joanbowling.com.

My dad was in charge of us kids for the evening. And he decided to take us to some place we had never been. Of course, I was three years old at the time; that's a mighty broad list of options.

We arrived at this plain, beige metal building that looked like nothing special. In fact, it looked downright dull and boring. I couldn't understand why people were lined up to go inside. We joined in at the end of that really long line. It was probably only five people but hey, I was only three; I had the attention span of a flea. When we finally made it up to the front of the line, my dad slipped some money through a window, and the electric buzzer unlocked and opened a giant door. I knew something great was going to happen. And my three-year-old eyes could not believe what I was seeing.

This place was like a palace to a small child. It had shag carpeting on the walls. A large, glittering disco ball spun its magic spell overhead. And people were gliding by effortlessly with wheels strapped on their feet. This was the most magical and wonderful place I had ever seen - the roller-skating rink!

At that moment, I knew that this was what I wanted to do for the rest of my life. I wanted to skate. And I wanted to be decked, head to toe, in glitter at all times.

So, I decided that I was going to figure this skating bit out and I was going to dedicate myself to it. Somehow or another, I was going to learn to skate just like all of the older kids and adults. They made it look so graceful. I, however, resembled a tiny baby deer with skates strapped to her feet. It didn't matter though. I got my first pair of skates and the challenge would be met. I skated all of the time and anywhere and everywhere I could.

Now, my parents couldn't always take me to the rink, so my mom was nice enough to put these big, thick plastic runners throughout the house so that I could skate inside. It was a really bold and fancy design choice in the 1970s. As long as I stayed on the runners, all was well and family peace was maintained.

I skated outside. I skated at school. I skated at friends' houses. I went back to the rink and skated some more. It was all I wanted to do. I did just that for many years.

And then, there came a point where they decided that I should be paired with someone else to skate. Now, there is a time in your life when you really do know it all. And I as a teenager, this was my time. "Absolutely not. I am not doing that. No way. You have got to be kidding me."

I gave up skating and left the roller rink. I found other things to do. I stayed busy through high school and college. I missed skating though, and I would daydream about it. I would sometimes go out to the roller rink and wonder what would have happened if I had not quit skating. Then something very special happened. They decided to open an ice rink in my own town.

"Hey, I should go try this out. This might be that special opportunity that I'm looking for."

I went out to the ice rink and I stood in line. The line stretched all the way around the building because, in my southern hometown, people were quite fascinated with the thought of an ice rink as many of the residents had never seen one in person. I waited patiently in line. When I reached the front of the line, I slipped my money through the window. The doors opened and I stepped into a new world. Once in the rink, the cold air hit me in the face and I thought, "Holy cow! It's cold in here!" Roller skating did not prepare me for that.

But, I saw the beautiful sheet of ice and the people effortlessly gliding past. The disco ball spun overhead, casting a sparkly spell across the ice. And I thought, "You know what - I've got this. I know how to roller skate. How hard could this be?"

Well, let me tell you something. When you fall, ice is really hard. And I fell a lot. I fell on my butt, on my knees, and on my elbows. I whacked my head a couple of times. But, I was going to figure out how to ice skate if it killed me. It nearly did, but I continued to work at it. I worked really hard.

I practiced. I tested. I competed. And I was rewarded. I received lots of medals, three of which are world medals. I'm very proud of those. I continued to skate through illness, injury, shows, competitions, and newly minted friendships. My professional life and personal life moved around my rink life for many years. But then I thought, "There must be something else I'm missing here."

As if I'd just asked the Universe to bring me something, the phone rang. It was a friend of mine from the rink who was a coach. She was starting an adult synchronized skating team. She was calling all the adults that she knew to see if she could get enough people to form a team and wanted to know if I would join.

Now, there might be some of you out there you don't know what synchronized skating is. It's a team of approximately 10 to 15 people who stay connected to each other at all times and skate at a very high rate of speed with sharp implements strapped on their feet. I mean, what could go wrong?

"Sure, I'd love to join the team; count me in."

Our first season, we worked really hard and we were rewarded. We received a sectional bronze medal; it was practically unheard of for a new team. We did the same thing our second year with another sectional bronze medal. We had a blast!

We had several more successful seasons as a team. Everybody was having a very good time. I'm not going to pretend that we didn't have our problems. We were like a family, with a few personality clashes and squabbles from time to time. Just imagine what it's like trying to get nearly 16 ladies to agree to wear the same dress and makeup to skate to one music selection. Consensus was not our strength, but giving our individual opinions on everything synchro related became commonplace.

What had been a team was becoming an on-ice convention of nagging volunteer coaches, content to call out what everyone else was doing wrong. Unchecked, this sparked a lot of problems and a lot of unnecessary drama.

I decided that I would take a break from synchronized skating so I could focus on my singles skating. I wanted to test up level and work a little bit harder. That year, our rink didn't have a synchro team because there weren't enough people. It was kind of nice and it was relaxing to not have these little bickering moments. But I missed my teammates.

And, there was another call again. The coach called to let me know that she was starting another team and she would really like for me to strongly consider being a part of it. I was unsure about being on a team. Being Catholic and highly schooled in the art of guilt, I decided that I didn't want to shoulder the responsibility of being the person who kept the team one member shy of being able to form a team for the season. I was going to be a synchro skater again.

It was a personal sacrifice for me to join the team that season. After an overly full day of work, I would skate with my coach for an hour. During that hour, my coach would not let me rest for a moment or slack in any way. She's fierce like that. After skating an hour with her, I would then get in the car, drive across town, and spend two and a half hours with my synchro team. And the next morning, I would get up and I would start my day at the ice rink again at 6AM. It was utterly exhausting.

It was worth it. We were a team.

As the season wore on, I noticed that I was starting to feel irritated with some of my teammates. They were missing practices, they didn't know the steps, and they didn't seem to care. Heck, we had one person who couldn't seem to remember to wear pants to practice! What kind of life must you have that pants are optional? If I had that life, I would not care about being on a synchro team.

I started to realize that perhaps maybe this is not what I wanted to do anymore. Maybe I just wanted to skate, but I was going to finish the season and I wanted to finish it strong. During our last run-through of our program before the holiday break, we ran our program with the intent of giving it our all. And, just a few seconds into the program, "BAM!" That was the sound of my head hitting the ice. And, as I rolled over quickly to try to catch up with the team, I saw the team skating off down the ice. I was wondering how I was going to catch them.

I had a realization. Maybe I don't want to catch them. Maybe I don't want to do this anymore. Maybe I don't want to skate.

I had yet another serious head injury to add to my résumé. A friend of mine pointed out to me, "You always seem to be injured." As I thought about that remark, I realized I was always injured from something that happened in synchro and it was taking me away from what I really enjoyed.

After the holidays, I came back and skated with the team for a few weeks. We had our big sectional competition coming up. Typically, at the last practice before the competition, everyone's nerves are high. This practice was no different. Teammates were getting on each other's nerves, driving one another crazy, and bickering was rampant. My teammates were telling me that I didn't know where I skated; I didn't know where my spot was. I had skated in that spot all season and it was as if they had forgotten that I had even been there. I thought, "I don't really feel like part of the team anymore. I don't feel like I'm even part of this group. This team didn't even check on me once while I was out and injured."

As that dawned on me, I realized I didn't care about finishing the season. I didn't even want to be there that night. I left. I left the team. I left the rink. And, as I walked out the door to the rink and into the dark parking lot, I was pretty certain I had left skating. It was over and I didn't even care.

I supported the team through the rest of their season, quietly, and cheered them on from the stands at sectionals. And when that season came to a close, I decided I should go back to the rink. I didn't really want to, but I knew that I should, for the sake of closure. I wanted to see if I was really done; if I was completely over ever skating again.

I went back to the rink and had to stand in line. It felt familiar, but this time I had zero excitement or expectation. I paid my money and when I walked through that open door, the smell of the rink rushed to greet me. Now, you're probably wondering: how does an ice rink smell? It smells like frozen mold; it's not exciting.

But, when you're a skater, it's one of the best things ever. It smells like home.

As I saw people glide past me, I wanted to get out on the ice. And, as I got out there on the ice and started skating, I realized what I enjoyed most. I realized that I enjoyed my skating. I realized that this was my passion and my commitment. I realized I had sacrificed that to help someone else out and that I'd continued to do that because I'd invested so much in it.

At this point, I chose to invest in myself. I invested in my skating and found my place of joy and wonder again. I didn't want anyone to ever take that away. Like the sparkly spell cast by the disco ball so many years ago, the magic was back!

Many business owners struggle with maintaining and growing their business, but business growth doesn't have to feel impossible. Angela L. Edwards is passionate about helping entrepreneurs and small businesses become more strategic, productive, and profitable. Using her unique CASTLE methodology, Angela works with businesses to produce immediate results.

Angela is the Chief Project Management Geek and Founder of Castle Thunder Consulting©. With 20 years of experience of managing difficult and impossible projects, Angela can show business owners how to apply project management principles to bring organization to chaotic processes, projects, and environments. Project Management isn't just a profession, it's a mindset that can be applied to help anyone identify, understand, and address key tasks in a methodical and practical manner.

As a figure skater, Angela learned that achieving goals isn't always an easy, straightforward process. She has navigated around a myriad of challenges that have fostered her attitude that nothing is impossible. It was this attitude that lead her to becoming a world gold medalist.

Angela graduated from Virginia Commonwealth University with a Bachelor of Science in Psychology. She also earned multiple graduate degrees from Strayer University, a Master of Business Administration and a Master of Science in Information Technology. Her professional certifications include Project Management Professional (PMP)®, Agile Certified Practitioner

(PMI-ACP) ®, Professional Certified Coach (PCC) ©, and Six Sigma Black Belt Professional (SSBBP)®.

For more information, visit www.castlethunder.com.

# References

**The Queen of the Second Row**

Rambo Research and Consulting is the copyright of Rambo Research and Consulting LLC.

**The Next Hundred Yards**

http://www.ironman.com/#axzz5LiWhWzAF

The IRONMAN® Triathlon is a registered trademark of World Triathlon Corporation.

This independent publication has not been authorized, endorsed, sponsored or licensed by, nor has content been reviewed or otherwise approved by, World Triathlon Corporation dba IRONMAN®.

DorothyErlanger.com is the copyright of Dorothy Erlanger.

**The 24-Hour Woman**

Cosmopolitan magazine is a trademark of World Triathlon Corporation.

Playboy magazine is a trademark of Playboy Enterprises, Inc.

Playgirl magazine was a trademark of Magna Publishing Group, Inc.

YolandaGray.com is the copyright of Yolanda Gray.

**How Did I Get Here?**

FABWomen is a copyright of FABWOMEN LLC.

**Searching for Treasure**

Successful Life Sailing with Captain Jim Gordon is a copyright of Jim Gordon.

**Have You Been to Selma Today?**

Crime TV and The Crime + Investigation television channel are the trademarks of A&E Television Networks LLC.

Rejoice Radio is the copyright of Richmond WREJ.

Women-On-Point and WCLM Radio are the copyright of Voices from the Drum (VFTD) 2016- 2018.

"Viola Gregg Liuzzo Biography," *Biography,* Bio and A&E Networks. https://www.biography.com/people/viola-gregg-liuzzo-370152.

Bio and the Bio logo are registered trademarks of A&E Television Networks, LLC.

ShirleyT.com is the copyright of Esteem Institute, LLC.

## The Gift of Africa

Season 5, Episode 206, "Out of Africa," *ER*, originally broadcast on NBC (US), 2003.

ElizabethLouis.com is the copyright of Elizabeth Louis.

## What Makes a House a Home

Reese's Peanut Butter Cups are a trademark of the Hershey Chocolate & Confectionery Corporation.

CVS Pharmacy is a trademark of the CVS Pharmacy, Inc.

People magazine is a trademark of the Meredith Corporation.

Listerine is a trademark of Warner Lambert Company LLC, a division of Johnson & Johnson Services, Inc.

BJ's is a trademark of BJ's Restaurants, Inc.

Toastmasters is a copyright of Toastmasters International.

TedX is a copyright of TED Conferences, LLC.

JoanBowling.com is the copyright of Joan Bowling Presents LLC.

## Wonderland

PMP® and PMI-ACP® are registered trademarks of the Project Management Institute, Inc.

Professional Certified Coach or PCC is a license designation through the International Coach Federation.

Six Sigma Black Belt Professional (SSBBP)® is a trademark of the Management and Strategy Institute.

Castle Thunder Consulting is a copyright of Castle Thunder Consulting LLC.

www.ingramcontent.com/pod-product-compliance
Lightning Source LLC
Chambersburg PA
CBHW052115070526
**44584CB00017B/2498**